Foundations for Measuring Quality in a Lawn

Mowing Business

Paul Fillmore

Acknowledgements

My wife is amazing. It would be impossible to be as happy as I am without her.

Table of Contents

Abstract

Measuring quality for a service industry can seem

daunting because the measurements seem very

subjective and there are a lot of aspects to consider

when measuring quality in mowing lawns. From the

perspective of the service provider, this paper

proposes that a quality begins with a quality

management plan. Other company functions, such as

collecting and incorporating customer requirements,

training, equipment maintenance, and self-

assessment, both support and provide very important

injects to the quality management program. It is

through this foundation that a lawn mowing company

can begin to define its standards for quality and

measure itself against those standards. This paper

does not propose the standards because those are

variables dependent upon numerous factors. Rather,

by establishing a quality management program with

the right supporting programs and injects, the company can build a firm foundation for setting a standard and assessing quality.

Introduction

In any organization, there must be some way to measure and assess the work accomplished. What is the standard and who is to say the mowed lawn meets some standard? Should the cut grass be 4 inches long or 3 inches? If the grass is 3.9 inches long, did the company fail to deliver quality? Additionally, not every blade of grass gets cut. So, what is an acceptable percentage of cut grass? Furthermore, if the grass looks great, but the technician injured himself by unsafe mowing practices, can the quality honestly be rated high? Safety standards should absolutely be incorporated into quality standards. When it comes to mowing lawns, the company should have some organizational structure and defined processes for measuring the quality of service provided. It is the structured program that will provide consistency over time and ensure an enduring posture of quality assurance.

A quality control framework will have multiple inputs or supporting functions, including the customer requirements, a training program, an equipment maintenance program, and ability to process feedback and implement changes.

A very important input is the customer's desires or requirements. No two customers are the same, so the quality control framework must allow for some input from the customer. One customer may want the grass cut shorter than another, or one may want the grass kept pristine every day of the week, when another customer may like the grass looking more natural. Therefore, any measure of quality must include the input from the customer.

The company must invest in training employees. Through a well-designed training program, the company will deliver competent and valued employees to the worksite. They will properly represent the company and perform to the company's quality standards.

Equipment maintenance is indispensable for a lawn mowing business. Poorly maintained equipment will detract from quality both by reflecting a unsatisfactory image of the company and substandard appearance of the grass.

Finally, the company must have a means to accept input and critically analyze itself. It should have a mechanism for processing feedback, identifying solutions, and incorporating those solutions.

Through these steps, a lawn mowing company can establish a quality management plan that provides the ability to assess the quality of service delivered.

4

Quality Management Program

A quality management program is not meant to be an onerous, bureaucratic nuisance, void of any substance. It should be a vibrant program that fits with the character and vision of the company. It should be a natural part of the culture of the organization. In Good to Great, Collins (2001) devotes a chapter to a culture of discipline, which can be applied to a quality management program. "Avoid the bureaucracy and hierarchy and instead create a culture of discipline" (Collins, 2001, p. 121). With this in mind, a structured program for quality must be the outgrowth of the company culture...otherwise, the program will fail to achieve what it is intended to achieve. Consider a department full of employees who enjoy socializing. Suppose they have a culture in their department of socializing and they produce little meaningful work products because they are so busy chatting, going on coffee breaks, enjoying mid-morning walks, and taking extended lunches together. If someone in that group decided to implement a program to measure their timeliness, it would be meaningless because the department has no culture of timeliness. It is not within that department's nature to care about timeliness, so the program would fail. Similarly, a quality management program will fail at a company that does not care about quality or has no culture for quality.

"A quality control program must meet the specific needs of the landscape firm" (Pennisi & Chance, 2013). For a business that focuses on lawn mowing only and not on the broader topic of landscaping, defining quality can be challenging. At a minimum, the company should consider "excellence of services rendered and/or good value provided for the price paid" (Pennisi & Chance,

2013). In developing a program, some structure must be established, including position descriptions that identify quality management responsibilities within each position. "Quality starts with the manager/owner" (Pennisi & Chance, 2013). The manager or owner should have a clear understanding of how quality is nested within the company's mission and vision, otherwise the company will be adrift producing inconsistent results and behaving erratically. It is the manager who will set the tone for quality and emphasize its importance to the rest of the staff and crew. If he does not assert the importance of quality, the employees will not see it as important, resulting in sloppy work, inconsistent service delivery, and an unprofessional workforce.

The next critical position is the quality manager, who tries to answer the question "'Does our delivery match our quality control policy?'" (Pennisi

& Chance, 2013). In answering this question, the quality manager will use a checklist to assess the quality of the service. This assessment is known as a quality control inspection (QCI). In a small company, the quality manager may also be the operations manager or the owner. In selecting someone for this position, it is best if the quality manager position is filled by an individual who does not actually mow the grass. In general, a person should not conduct a QCI on his own work because that would be a conflict of interest. The quality manager "has no operational or sales role and reports directly to the company president, lending credence to his objectivity" (Chilcote, 2011). However, it is very important that the quality manager be involved in the planning, organizing, delivery, and close-out of the service. By involving the quality manager in the beginning of the service, quality is underscored as an important aspect of the service. Additionally, the quality manager will be able to provide valuable input and guidance throughout the project. He may identify issues during the planning phase that will impact the quality of the work. He can also identify current deficiency trends and offer recommendations to eliminate problem areas. The quality manager is an important role, indispensable to a quality management program.

The next critical position is the person who actually performs the service…in this case, the person who mows the lawn. Ideally, that individual will believe in the culture and vision for the company. However, that is not always the case. Even when the technician who mows the grass does not have a mindset for quality work, he can still deliver the quality demanded by the company. He can be trained to deliver quality work, and his work can be inspected, then corrected when needed. Training is an integral part of a quality management program, and the specifics of training will be discussed later in this paper.

Finally, safety is a critical component of quality. Although a site safety and health officer is a real position in many companies, these duties can be handled by the operations manager or quality manager in a smaller company. More importantly, a culture of safety is indispensable. Pennisi and Chance (2013) claim that "safety is quality control in one of its purest forms." Some companies give the appearance of adhering safe work practices, but do not have a safety mindset or culture. There are companies that post Occupational Safety and Health Administration signs and placards, hold perfunctory safety meetings, and give the appearance of a safe work environment, but deliberately engage in unsafe work practices when nobody is looking. The employees work on overhead projects without a bump cap as the supervisor keeps watch for a safety Nazi. Or a technician works from the top step of a step ladder rather than get a ladder of proper height for the task. Such companies do not have a culture of safety. In the lawn mowing business, no weeds or grass or overgrown ditch is worth jeopardizing someone's health, limb, or life. There is no high mark for quality that can mitigate a team member becoming injured or hospitalized to achieve such high quality. Therefore, a quality management program should align perfectly with the safety program.

A properly run safety program includes safety equipment. Personal protective equipment, such as the right boots, hearing and eye protection, proper clothing to protect from the sun or elements, and

gloves should be made available to the employees.
Not only should the equipment be provided, but it
should be regularly inspected to ensure it can provide
the protection it is supposed to. Any damaged or
worn-out equipment should be properly disposed of
and replaced. The proper equipment is only one facet
of safety, while training is another. Some of the
specifics about safety will be further discussed in the
Training section.

Customer Input

Although this paper describes quality from the perspective of the service provider, the company's quality management program cannot be completely decoupled from the customer's desires. A quality management program must have an avenue to receive input from the customer. The intent is not to make the customer the quality manager or employ the customer as the person conducting the quality control inspection. The goal is to receive the customer's desires for his lawn. The reason is quite simple...because the customer sets the requirements. The mower has a variable deck height, so the grass can be cut at any length to suite the customer. Some grass should be left longer, while other grass can be cut shorter. Some customers may want the clippings bagged and removed from the property while others want the clippings to remain in the lawn. These desires from the customer become benchmarks for the company to measure quality. The quality control checklist would become an individualized checklist for each property because it would include items specifically requested by the customer. For example, one line item may simply read, "Mower height set at 3.5" per customer's request...yes or no". Other customer requirements include frequency of cutting the grass, direction, which areas require a push mower or should be left untouched, time of day or days of week authorized for mowing, or restrictions on where the truck and trailer can be parked. All these requirements come from the customer, are processed by the company, then should be made items on the quality control inspection checklist.

There may be instances when the customer's desires do not align with our company goals, standards, capability, or regulations. For example, if the customer wants the grass cut too short and it will burn the grass, the operations manager may need to intervene and reach an agreement with the customer that falls within the company's standards for a well presented lawn. Similarly, if a customer's property is in Winter Garden and wants it mowed before 7:00am, the company would need to inform the customer that the requirement is in violation of Article IV of Chapter 38 Section 155 of Winter Garden City code and cannot be met. The customer would have to agree to an alternate time that is allowed by the city. Another customer may want the grass mowed with a mulching blade. Meeting that requirement would be dependent on whether or not the company has a mower with a mulching blade.

"Conducting a survey of customer needs in the form of a short questionnaire (one to two pages) may help you fine-tune and manage their expectations and your delivery" (Pennisi & Chance, 2013). To discuss requirements with the customer, the company should send an experienced person who is knowledgeable about grass, local regulations, and the equipment used by the company.

Training

Employees need training in two broad areas: equipment and company policies. For the equipment, they must be taught about the capabilities of the equipment, trained how to use and perform basic maintenance, and trained how to properly store the equipment. They must also be assessed to determine how effective the training was, ideally before they are sent to a jobsite. The training should cover a myriad to topics, including how to adjust the equipment to accommodate the customer's requirements (such as deck height), when to use a push mower rather than a riding mower, pre-checks prior to operating equipment, procedures in the event of equipment malfunction, how to disable hydraulics to push a zero-turn mower, indications that the blade needs sharpening, etc. Ensuring the employees understand the equipment capabilities and how they operate so they can provide the best cut possible. Different decks and different blade heights have an impact on the grass and are a factor when the customer wants the grass left longer than most. "It is important to mow with a deck that emphasizes airflow management under the deck to avoid simply pushing the grass over. High-lift blades combined with excellent airflow management ensure grass blades stand up to be cut at the correct height — delivering that after-cut appearance customers are looking for" (Dowdle, 2013). It is also important for the employees to understand when to cut the grass short and when to leave it a bit longer. "One very common mistake is mowing lawns too short. Lawns mowed at higher heights tend to have deeper roots, less weed problems, and look much better. Mowing too close invites problems such as weed invasions" ("Guidelines for Mowing", n.d.).

Within the category of equipment training, the employees would receive training on personal protective equipment. This training would cover all possible personal protective equipment; requirements or regulations for what must be worn; and proper donning, wear, and storage or disposal. Proper use of personal protective equipment is also a safety matter, which is a very important component of quality.

Training should also include company policies, including the quality management program. They should be taught about the foundation of the program, starting with the company's mission and vision, then how the quality management program supports that mission and vision. They must understand their role in the process. A quality manager has a different role than a technician who mows the grass. Both will interface with the customer, but the technician really doesn't have much authority to negotiate with the customer. So, the technician must understand the limits of his authority, how to handle challenging customers, and when to call the quality or operations manager. Another facet of training is how to handle accidents, such as damaging the lawn, bushes or trees, sidewalk, driveway, breaking a window, or backing over a mailbox. All these accidents are real possibilities for which both the technician and company management must be prepared to handle. Additionally, the technician should be trained on personal appearance standards, friendliness, attitude, and company image. Interaction with other employees and coworkers also impacts quality. "Customers often note the way the employees treat each other, especially boss - worker relationships" (Pennisi & Chance, 2013).

There are a myriad of topics to cover in employee training and this paper has touched on a handful that have direct impact on quality. A

company that follows a solid training program,

tightly aligned with the quality management program,

will enhance its ability to consistently deliver high

quality lawn mowing service.

Equipment Maintenance

Equipment comes with a recommended maintenance schedule that should be closely followed. Properly maintaining the equipment will ensure the warranty remains valid. Well-maintained equipment also performs better, lasts longer, and enables the crew to work as effectively and efficiently as possible. Maintaining equipment starts with the obvious tasks, such as keeping blades sharp. "A good question to weed out low quality lawn care providers: 'How often do you sharpen your blades?'" (Birket, 2014). A sharp blade is very important because it "gives the lawn an even appearance and reduces disease from damage caused by a dull mower blade" (Guidelines for Mowing Lawns, n.d.). Beside sharp blades, engine maintenance is crucial. The oil should be changed regularly, air filters should be checked and changed when needed, rotating assemblies should be kept lubricated, and safety features should be kept in good condition. Finally, equipment should be kept clean because a neat appearance enhances the company image which has a direct impact on quality. Pennisi and Chance (2013) list vehicle appearance and correct parking as items to consider for a quality control checklist.

Feedback Loop

A company must be able to change. Within the quality management program, there must be a mechanism to analyze feedback or inspection reports, identify solutions to issues, and make meaningful changes to techniques, procedures, or company policy. There are several pathways for input. The quality control checklist provides information. Other information injects include customer feedback, employee feedback, observations from third parties, changes in local regulations, or updates to industry standards. The company must be able to process the information, develop any changes or updates, implement solutions, update applicable policies, and update the quality management plan accordingly. This topic also includes trend analysis. For example, if the technician is reporting the mower cutting unevenly, maintenance records may indicate a recurring issue every 300 hours of use. An

investigation may find that a couple of nuts require

thread lock after servicing. An update to

maintenance procedures would add thread lock to

those items, which would extend the maintenance

cycle of the equipment, improve its effectiveness, and

positively impact quality. Similarly, customer

appreciation of a particular employee, or consistently

high customer satisfaction for one employee may

mean he is ready for promotion to quality manager.

There are countless scenarios of feedback to a

company. Regardless of the source, the company

needs to be open to receiving the feedback,

processing it, then acting upon what it learns. The

ability to change is imbedded in the company culture

and has a direct impact on quality management.

Conclusion

In order to measure quality in a lawn mowing business, the company must first develop a quality management program that supports the mission and vision of the company and is consistent with the company's culture. The program will include position descriptions, duties and responsibilities of each position and an integrated safety program. Other organizational functions have a direct impact on quality. Those functions include soliciting customer requirements, a training program for employees, and equipment maintenance. Finally, the company must be able to receive feedback and inspection results, identify lessons learned, determine solutions, and incorporate changes into company procedures.

References

Birkett, A. (2014, October 22). 7 Things To Look

For When Hiring A Lawn Care Company.

Retrieved from

https://www.lawnstarter.com/blog/lawn-care-

industry/7-things-look-hiring-lawn-care-

company/

Chilcote, L. (2011, May26). Quality Control.

Retrieved from

http://www.lawnandlandscape.com/article/ll-

052611-bemus-landscape-quality-control/

Collins, J. (2001). *Good to Great*. New York, NY:

HarperCollins.

Dowdle, L.H. (2013, June 24). How to Balance

Mower Speed & Quality Cut. Retrieved from

https://www.totallandscapecare.com/how-to-

landscape/balancing-act/

30

Guidelines for Mowing Lawns Properly. (n.d.). In

    *Lawntalk.*Retrieved May 5, 2018, from

    http://extension.illinois.edu/lawntalk/planting/

    guidelines_for_mowing_lawns.cfm

Pennisi, B., & Chance, W. (2013, July). Landscape

    Basics:Designing a Quality Control Program

    for Your Company. Athens, Ga: The

    University of Georgia.